SHOULD YOU WORK FROM HOME?

THE TRUTH ABOUT REMOTE WORK & HOW TO
FIND REAL REMOTE JOBS FAST!

JENNIFER JELLIFF-RUSSELL

EVERGROWTH COACH LLC

CONTENTS

INTRODUCTION

If you're reading this book, it's because you're either thinking about dipping your toes into the work from home lifestyle, or you're interested in learning how to find a better remote position than the one you already have. Either way, I'm so excited to help you in your journey!

There are a number of reasons you might be looking for a remote position. As I write this book, the world is experiencing a pandemic which has affected many organizations' abilities to continue working in an office environment. This book will touch on how Covid-19 has shifted, not only how people think about remote work, but also how the virus has impacted the process of searching for remote positions.

While the latter part of this book's purpose is to help you effectively find and apply for remote employment opportunities both now and after the pandemic, the first section will help you determine if remote work is actually a good fit for you or not.

You see, some people thrive in a remote work environment and, as we'll discuss later, can actually get *more* done while working from home than they did in a traditional office setting.

When I first switched to working remotely, I was doing the same job (with the same company) that I had done in a traditional office setting. I was excited to drop the forty-five minute daily commute and really looked forward to not having to get quite as dressed up as when I worked in the office. I had also worked in the same office as the director of my department and thought I'd get some relief from the stress of being "on" all the time. That maybe by switching to remote work, I'd be able to cut myself a little bit of slack and take the occasional break to wander down to the kitchen for a snack or walk the dogs in the middle of the day.

It only took one week of working from home to realize that the only thing about remote work that I'd gotten right was that I didn't have to drive to the office anymore! I'd fallen prey to believing in several of the myths listed in Section One of this book. I was very lucky though and, when I recognized that I was struggling in a position I'd previously excelled at while in a traditional office, I was able to get tips from several co-workers who were also remote employees. Because of their suggestions (which I include at the end of this book), rather than struggling for months before I got the hang of working from home, I was instead able to shift my way of thinking about remote work, got myself (and my home office) organized, and ended up being one of the top performers across both in-office and remote employees on the team.

Had I not had their guidance to help, I might have continued struggling for months before figuring things out on my own. Which is one of the reasons I decided to write this book—to help people like you who want to thrive in a work from home position!

However, there's always a flip side to the coin. Many of the issues I struggled with when I initially switched to working from home were more organizational in nature rather than personality based. I tend to be more of an introvert, so working by myself in a home environment with limited interruptions was the perfect fit for my personality.

On the flip side of the introvert coin are those people who are extroverts. These folks tend to struggle to work effectively in a remote position because they need that social interaction that working in a traditional office brings.

Before I switched to remote work, one of my co-workers at that organization, let's call him Dan, was forced to switch to working from home in the same position when the company decided to close his office. Things seemed fine for Dan at first, but as an extrovert who recharged his energy by chatting with co-workers, Dan began to struggle when relegated to working by himself at home. His performance started to suffer and he found himself constantly on the phone with co-workers trying to fill that void of having other people around. In the long run, Dan ended up leaving the company and taking another position that offered a traditional office setting.

As you can see from Dan's example, some folks just don't do well with working from home. In Section One of this book, I'll go over which traits tend to help people excel in remote employment and which traits tend to cause employees to struggle when working from home. This will help you determine if remote employment is the best bet for you or not.

How to Use This Book

For those who are already working from home, some of this information might be obvious, and you may wish to jump straight to the sections on how to successfully search for and land your next remote job. For those who have not yet had a work from home position, I highly recommend reading this book cover to cover as it will help you gain a better grasp of what it really means to work remotely.

There are a lot of myths and misunderstandings out there about what working from home really entails. That's why this book will start with a section to explain just what work from home employment is...as well as what it isn't. In that section, you'll learn about all the myths about working from home as well as the potential pitfalls you might encounter in a remote position. You see, many applicants interested in working from home find that they've bought into some of the myths about remote employment and that the reality is not quite as glamorous as they'd hoped. Reading through the myths and pitfalls will help you determine if you'd be a good fit for a work from home position.

In Section Two, I'll focus on helping you find legitimate work from home opportunities. We'll focus mostly on free job search methods though I do include one paid job search website.

In Section Three, we'll dig into the specifics of how to effectively apply for a remote role. There you'll get guidance on the application process and how it's different from applying for in-person positions. We'll also go over how to build an effective cover letter as well as what you might do differently in a resume to show the hiring manager that you're a great fit for a work from home job.

Section Four will focus on helping you ace the interview

by preparing you for what will be different when interviewing for a remote job. This section is filled with tips for how to approach phone or video interviews as well as suggestions of best practices when answering the interviewer's questions.

And, lastly, we'll wrap up with Section Five where I'll provide you with some ideas for how to thrive in your new, remote job!

A quick note: If you're looking for detailed instructions for how to create a resume, build a professional LinkedIn profile, nail a job interview, or negotiate a salary, check out my more robust guide, Cut the Bullsh*t, Land the Job: A Guide to Resume Writing, Networking, Interviewing, LinkedIn, Salary Negotiation, and More!

Now, let's make sure we're on the same page with what I mean when I refer to "work from home" jobs in this book.

Work from Home Terminology

Though I will primarily use the term "work from home" throughout this book, I will also occasionally refer to working from home as "remote" or "virtual" work since these terms are interchangeable.

If you've already started searching for remote work, another term you might have heard is "gig work." However, gig work is a very different thing than what I mean when I refer to work from home positions.

With work from home positions, I am referring to roles that are full-time, part-time, or temporary that provide a steady paycheck and require you to work a set amount of hours each day. Gig work is different in that you only work when the company has a project or task for you to complete. The key difference here is that you get paid for the amount of hours worked with work from home or remote positions, but with gig work, you get paid per task or per project completed *regardless of the hours worked.*

I'm not anti-gig work. In fact, gig work can be a really great option for folks who are unable to work in traditional roles that require large chunks of dedicated time. Many gigs allow you to complete projects at your own pace or at whatever time of day works best for you. So, if you tend to be a night owl and are most productive in the wee hours of the morning, gig work might be beneficial for you since you can complete the work at any hour of the day.

If you can find gig work that you're really good at, then you might be able to complete projects or tasks quickly and thereby make more money in less time than a traditional position might allow. You could take on and complete multiple gigs a day, or accept a gig, complete it, and then take the rest of the day off.

There are definitely perks to focusing on gig work. However, there are some definite drawbacks as well. If it takes you a long time to complete the gig's project or task, then you might end up getting paid a lot less than you normally would from a traditional, hourly position.

A great example of gig work is resume writing. Let's say you sign up to write resumes for a company as a gig. You hop on the company site, take on a listed resume gig that pays $50 for a finished resume, and then get to work updating or creating the resume. If you can create and submit the finished resume in, let's say, two hours, great! You've just gotten paid $50 for only two hours of work—which breaks down to $25 an hour. Not bad! But, if it takes you five hours to finish the resume and make that same $50, then your time was only worth $10 an hour.

Besides gig work, another thing to be on the lookout for

are surveys. If you want to sign up for paid surveys, that's fine, just know it's not a job nor is it gig work. The way most paid surveys work is that you provide your personal information or opinion to a company and receive either monetary compensation or a gift card. Many survey companies have actually shifted to a points system. So, in order to get a gift card or earn a certain amount of money, you have to rack up a specific number of points first by completing surveys.

If these surveys were just your opinion on a product or service, I wouldn't be so wary of them; however, many surveys are actually just getting you to sign up for credit cards or other services.

Keep in mind that this book is geared toward helping you connect with more traditional employment that just happens to be remote. The suggested websites recommended in this guide will remain focused on that goal. If some of these sites list surveys or gig work next to remote employment, I'll make sure to give you a heads up.

Let's Get to It!

Now that you know a little more about what to expect from this book, let's dive in so you can decide if working from home is the right choice for you and then get started in your job search to land that coveted remote position!

1

WHAT REMOTE WORK REALLY ENTAILS

This is where a lot of job applicants tend to sabotage themselves. If you apply for remote jobs without fully knowing what a work from home position really entails, you might go through all the hard work of landing a position only to quit within the first week when it doesn't meet your expectations.

Only you can decide if a work from home position is right for you. However, let me help you make that decision by providing you with more information about the realities of working from home. Unfortunately, there are a lot of myths out there about what it means to actually work remotely. In this section, I'll focus first on dispelling some of the misinformation about working from home, share who tends to struggle and who tends to do well in a remote work environment, and then I'll go over some of the pitfalls of taking a remote job.

Let's start with the myths about work from home jobs.

Remote Work Myths

As an employment coach, one of the things that I frequently found myself doing was debunking some of the myths around the idea of working from home. See if you can spot a few that you've heard during your job search. Hopefully, none of these myths are the specific reason that you want to find remote employment.

Myth #1: You get to work in your pajamas

I can totally see why this is something people think about those who work from home. After all, there is a little bit of truth to it. For a few remote jobs, you don't have to dress up or even change out of your pajamas. However, those are few and far between. Most work from home positions require weekly or daily meetings just like an in-person role would. Just because you're on a video conference at home rather than sitting in the office conference room doesn't mean you don't have to wear the appropriate attire.

Covid Note: During the pandemic, many people suddenly found themselves working from home for the first time ever. While your boss might have been okay with you wearing pajamas during such a difficult time, employers with permanently remote roles typically expect their remote personnel to get dressed like any other employee going to work in an office environment.

As someone who has worked remotely for a traditional employer and worked from home as an entrepreneur, I find it very important to get dressed in the morning. Maintaining a morning routine similar to that from when I worked in an office environment allows me to separate my work life from my home life. It also helps ensure that I start work at the same time every morning. When I don't maintain a specific morning routine, it's very easy to let the things I enjoy doing (like reading and binge-watching the latest TV shows) bleed into my workday.

Myth #2: Remote work is easier than working in an office

I cannot stress enough how incorrect this is. While you might not have a supervisor nearby to make sure you're actually working, that doesn't mean you do less work. Or at least, it shouldn't. In fact, I found that when I went from working in a traditional office environment to working from home doing the exact same job for the same company, I actually worked *harder* while working remotely.

For me, this increase in productivity while working remotely was because I no longer got interrupted by co-workers popping by my cubicle. Because I was able to fully focus on each task without the interruptions, I was able to get a whole lot more accomplished each day. However, that also meant that I then rolled on to the next task much sooner than I would have when I was in a traditional office environment.

Something else to keep in mind regarding this myth is that employers with remote positions are not stupid. They know that some people think they won't actually have to do as much if they aren't in an office environment, so they put systems in place specifically to crack down on employees who might be shirking their workload.

When I first shifted to remote work, my supervisor initially checked in on me a little more often than he had when I worked in an office. He also kept an eye on my production numbers to ensure that they didn't slip when I transitioned to remote work.

Those are just two examples of how an employer can keep tabs on you. Other options include software that allows an employer to make sure their staff are doing what they're supposed to be doing. That software can tell your supervisor what websites you've visited, how much time you're spending on each task, and can also track your keyboard activity.

The bottom line is this: Employers are not paying you to sit around. They are paying you to work. So if you land a remote position, expect to work just as hard as those staff who are in an office environment.

Myth #3: You can watch your kids while doing remote work

This is a tricky one. After all, a remote position could be a great fit for a stay-at-home parent; however, this all depends on the type of job and how old your children are.

If you're a parent, you know that children are not great at sitting still or being quiet for eight hours straight. In fact, it seems that kids only really want your attention when you have something else going on. (Think about it. The last time you were on a call, did your child suddenly need something *right then* that they didn't need before you got on the phone?)

If your position requires you to be on the phone or in virtual meetings with customers or clients, that is not a very compatible role with also watching your child. And you might be thinking to yourself, *But my kid is a good kid and doesn't yell or scream while I'm on the phone.* Or *My child is young enough to sleep most of the day.*

That's great. But for the parents with babies, you know they are going to wake up at some point and when they do, there will be crying. Which means you'll need to step away from work to care for them. And, for those parents with young kids who are quiet, you know your child will still need your supervision during the day while you're working.

This doesn't mean you should rule out remote work entirely though! Instead, look for positions which don't require you to be on the phone with clients or customers. These could be roles like remote chat agent (so you're typing instead of talking with customers), transcriptionist, community moderator, copywriter... the list goes on and I've only focused on writing/typing heavy roles. If you have a specialty like graphic design, accounting, underwriting, or project management, then there are even more opportunities out there for you. You'll just have to keep in mind that some of these roles do still require a quiet environment for the occasional call with clients or managers.

If your goal to work from home is primarily because you have a young child in the house, I mainly recommend looking into gig work instead. It's a lot more flexible and would be a better fit for this situation since you could knock out tasks and projects whenever you have some free time.

Covid Note: If your regular office job just shifted to remote employment and your child's school is closed, then there isn't a whole lot of choice for you. You can either try and balance helping your child distance-learn while continuing to perform your job remotely, or you can consider looking for gig work that will allow you to work around your child's school schedule.

Myth #4: You can work from anywhere

Yes, technically, you can work anywhere that has the tools or resources you need (like high-speed internet or a phone line). However, some employers are pretty strict when it comes to allowing you to travel. For example, though I worked remotely for my last employer, I was not allowed to simply travel somewhere and continue to work. I actually signed an agreement that I would work from a specific location every day (and that the location I chose would have high speed, reliable internet).

This myth can really bite you in the butt. Just because you *can* work from anywhere, doesn't mean it will actually work out when you try it. When I first opened my career services business, I took a vacation that included a 12-hour car trip during which I worked on several resumes. (Don't worry, I wasn't the driver.)

Though I was able to complete all the resumes, I was constantly distracted by what was out the car window. It also ended up being trickier than I thought to find areas to stop and access the internet in order to send the completed resumes to clients. Sure, you could turn your phone into a hotspot, but if you encounter areas with zero coverage, then it can hamper your work a bit.

So while this one isn't a total myth, I would say if you plan to try and travel with your remote job, check with your employer to make sure they're okay with it and plan ahead to make sure that the places you'll be staying will have reliable internet access.

Myth #5: You can work when medically admitted to the hospital

This one is a pretty random and rare myth, but it is still out there. Working from home does not mean that if you are admitted to a hospital that you can continue working. The majority of employers view this as a liability for their organization and will most likely require you to take Family and Medical Leave (if it's an option at your work) or regular leave.

Myth #6: Remote jobs don't pay very well

While there are definitely remote opportunities out there that barely pay above minimum wage, it's really no different from the pay you'd find with a traditional in-office position. Pay or salary all depends on what type of job it is and your experience or education as related to that position.

That said, I have seen some organizations which pay a dollar or two less to their remote employees than they pay their in-office staff. My recommendation is to avoid working for those companies and focus on organizations who at least pay the average amount for your particular line of work. Just because you're working from home, does not mean you're doing less work (and, as stated in Myth #2, it's likely you'll actually accomplish more tasks in a remote position).

Myth #7: Customer service is the only type of remote work available

This is one I've heard a lot and I can see why people would feel that way. Customer service roles tend to make up the vast majority of remote positions because they are the easiest type of work for employers to monitor in a remote capacity. (Notice I did not say that customer service roles are the easiest job to do. In my opinion, customer service is one of the more difficult jobs, but I digress.)

You'll find that roles which include some kind of customer service aspect will pop up a lot more than other types of work during searches for remote employment.

However, they are not the only remote positions out there. In fact, with the technology we have today (that is evolving and advancing even as I type this!) most positions can now be done from home!

During the pandemic, a lot of industries found that they could shift their roles to remote and that their employees were just as productive as they were when commuting to the office every day. Because they were forced to think outside the box and ensure all tasks could still be completed remotely, they found that it was, indeed, possible for employees to work from home in positions for which that was previously considered impossible.

Even before the pandemic, many companies were discovering that by opening their positions to employees working from home, they then gained a larger group of qualified candidates to select from and thereby gained employees who were a better fit for the job and company.

Quite frankly, if a position doesn't require you to perform a task in person, then you'll likely find remote opportunities for it. You'll find remote position opportunities in information technology, social work, nursing, project management, design, marketing – the list goes on and on!

All it takes is a quick job search paired with the word "remote" on a job search site to see if there are remote positions available in your field. Why not take a look?

Will You Sink or Swim?

As mentioned in the introduction to this book, some of us really excel in a remote environment, working by ourselves with limited interactions and virtually no interactions unless we pick up the phone or hop on a video call. The question is: Are you the type of person who will thrive in this kind of environment?

Now that you've read through the myths of remote work, you have a better idea of what to expect (and what not to expect) when it comes to working from home. As such, you can probably guess what personality traits or strengths tend to help someone do well at working from home and which traits or strengths might lead someone to struggle in a remote role.

To help you decide if remote employment is a good fit for you, I've created a list of traits and strengths for those who tend to naturally excel in remote work. Keep in mind as you read through this list that, just because you might not have a natural tendency toward these strengths, does not mean that you can't get better at them and eventually master them.

Traits & Strengths that suggest you might excel at remote employment:

- I like to work alone
- I don't mind working for hours without talking to anyone
- I'm very organized
- I'm a self-starter
- I can complete projects without direct supervision
- I'm okay with asking for help
- I'm good at figuring things out on my own
- I'm good at communicating by phone, video, or email
- I'm not easily distracted (by social media, household chores, etc.)

- I'm good at maintaining my work schedule (stopping and starting at the same time each day)

As you read through the above list, ask yourself if any of these sound like you. Don't be discouraged if none of the above traits sounds like you! Remember, just because you might not exhibit these traits naturally, doesn't mean that you can't learn them over time.

When I initially started working from home, I really struggled to separate my work life from my personal life. It took a little time to get better at making myself stop working at the end of the day. Only after some trial and error did I figure out that setting reminders 15 minutes before the end of the day combined with leaving my work phone in my home office and closing the door at the end of the day were what I needed to do in order to stop working.

It's also possible to develop bad habits over time. I might have started out going 90 miles per hour when I first switched to remote employment, but after a year of working from home, I began to get distracted by household chores. I'd find myself running downstairs for a snack and pausing to start a load of laundry or do the dishes in between calls. These tasks weren't a huge timesuck, but as you'll see in the next section about pitfalls, falling into the habit of doing household chores while on the clock can be a slippery slope.

Just keep in mind when reading through that list of traits and strengths that if you don't exhibit *any* of them, that you might struggle a bit more than others at remote employment. But again, that doesn't necessarily mean that you can't do it. It just means that there will be a bit of a learning curve when you initially start a remote position.

What to Avoid in a Remote Position

While there are plenty of perks to working from home, there are also a few pitfalls to try and avoid. Some of them you'll recognize as echoing from the previous sections on myths about working from home, and others you might not recognize until you've fallen into the bad habit.

A really great mantra to keep in mind is that if you wouldn't do something in a traditional office setting, then you probably shouldn't do it while working from home.

So, with that in mind, here are some things to avoid in a remote position.

Pitfall #1: Not having a set work schedule

Ironically, while some people think that you'll work less while in a remote work position, the truth is that you actually end up working more! For me, it was partially because I couldn't seem to stop working at the end of the day. It was so easy to just read one more email or tackle one more task. After all, I no longer had the commute home, so what did it matter if I took a few extra minutes at the end of the day to complete a project?

The problem was that these extra few minutes slowly morphed into an extra hour or more of work every night because I just couldn't stop working. I eventually had to set an alarm to alert me to when it was 15 minutes until the end of my workday. Then I got into the routine of taking that 15 minutes to make a to-do list for the next day. It made it a lot easier to stop working if I could put a sort of "bookmark" in my day by creating my to-do list where I would pick up my task the next day.

Another thing I did was to turn off my work phone at the

end of the day. Here's the thing: when you work in an office environment, you don't answer work calls after hours, right? So why should you answer work-related calls after hours just because you're working remotely? Since my supervisor and co-workers had my personal number, if there was an emergency, they would still have been able to reach me.

The best thing you can do for keeping your personal life and work life separate in a remote position is to first set a schedule of when you'll start and stop working. Most of the time, your employer will tell you what hours you'll work, but there are some positions which allow you to choose your hours of work. I recommend setting your work hours and sticking to them.

Pitfall #2: Working wherever

It can be tempting to work in a different part of your house each day just to keep things interesting. The downside of moving around is that it's hard to get into "work mode" if you're constantly adjusting to a new environment. There's also the issue that you'll likely be leaving work paraphernalia all over your house instead of having it in a dedicated spot. Maintaining a space dedicated just to your remote work allows you to be more organized. This also means that you'll be able to find work-related items more quickly instead of searching all over your home for them.

I'm lucky that I have a space in my house dedicated specifically to working from home. It's an office with a door that I can close at the end of the day. This is really helpful in creating boundaries between work and my personal life. I can leave my work phone in that office at the end of the day, close the door, and go downstairs.

If you don't have a dedicated office, you can instead

identify a specific space like a side table to keep your work separate from your home life. And if that's also not an option, then I personally think it's worth taking that last 10 minutes each evening to pack your work-related equipment away (if possible) and stow it out of sight. Yes, that means you'll have to get it back out every morning, but it's worth it if it means you're not checking your work emails at 10pm because the computer was right there.

I also recommend that you avoid working from your bed since it sends a mixed message to your brain. Rather than thinking that it's time to relax when you go to bed at night, your brain might instead think that it's time to go into work mode. However, I also know that the reality is that sometimes a bed is all the space you have to work with. In that case, as mentioned above, I do recommend packing your computer and any other work equipment away each night so it is out of sight.

Pitfall #3: Getting drop-in visitors or calls

This can be one of the more difficult aspects of working from home. Especially if you have friends or family members who don't understand that when you say that you're working from home, that you're actually working!

Remember, if you wouldn't do it at an office, then I don't recommend doing it at home. Does that mean you can't ever answer personal calls while working? No, of course not. But if one of your long-winded friends or family members calls you expecting to chat for a few hours, then you shouldn't answer their call during work hours. Let it go to voicemail then call them back after hours or during a lunch break, just as you would at a regular office job.

Pitfall #4: Household chores

I have absolutely fallen into this trap. You start out thinking, *Well, I have five minutes. I'll just throw in a load of laundry. It's no big deal, right?* The problem is that this kind of thing tends to snowball. Suddenly, you're taking a longer lunch break to do the dishes. Or taking advantage of the fact that you're home alone to mop the floors.

If you're going to clock out and clock back in to do these things, then it's not an issue. Consider it like leaving the office to run a quick personal errand. Most office roles would require that you clock out for such a personal trip. In the same vein, I recommend clocking out if you're going to do household chores during the day.

A caveat to this is that if the chore is necessary to you actually being able to do your work, then it's okay to do. For example, if you need to take some time to organize your workspace because you can't find some paperwork you need, then it's okay to do that during work hours.

An odd example of this that I've personally run into is that I heat my home with a wood stove during the winter. I once had to make a quick trip to our woodshed outside to get another load of wood during the workday because I'd run out and the house was getting too cold to continue working. Of course, the moment I stepped out, one of the executives of my organization called! I had to call him back and explain that I didn't answer my phone because I had to go bring in firewood. Luckily, he thought it was hilarious and understood that it was a necessary task so that I could continue working without freezing.

While on the clock, try to only complete tasks that are related to your job. Otherwise, if you're doing personal stuff while on the clock, your employer might consider it as stealing (since you're getting paid to be working).

Pitfall #5: Running personal errands during work

Just like you wouldn't do household chores at work if you were in an office environment, you also wouldn't leave your desk to run personal errands without clocking out first. If there's something that you absolutely must go do, make sure to let your supervisor know and ask if you need to clock out or not for that task.

Some employers are more lenient than others, so it's possible that your employer won't care, but it's good to make sure of this before you get caught taking an hour off to go pick up a prescription when you're supposed to be working on a project.

Hopefully reading through these pitfalls and myths coupled with the information on what personality traits tend to thrive in a remote work environment will give you a better idea of whether working from home is a good fit for you or not.

2

HOW TO FIND A WORK FROM HOME JOB

The biggest issue with finding remote work is knowing what is a scam, what is gig work, and what is an actual remote job opportunity. In this section, we'll dig into those issues, as well as what to be on the lookout for in job descriptions. I'll then direct you to some great websites for finding remote opportunities. But before we jump into that, I want to address the elephant in the room for at least the first half of 2021.

As briefly mentioned earlier, Covid-19 has shifted the job search for remote employment. At the moment, the majority of positions currently listed across the United States are listed as remote or temporarily remote because many offices are closed. There are pros and cons to this. Let's take a look at both.

On the pros side, businesses closing their offices actually opens up some opportunities you might not have had before. Companies that have never allowed remote employment are suddenly allowing anyone to apply for positions, regardless of where the applicant is located. This means you could potentially have a shot at temporary work with a company with offices on the other side of the country without having to relocate. Just keep in mind that it's likely to be a temporary role unless you're willing to relocate once their office reopens. However, that short time with the organization could be a real help not only on your wallet, but also in giving you more experience, thus building out your resume with more skills.

There is also the possibility that the organization might decide that they love your work as an employee and want to keep you at their organization even it means you're one of the only remote employees. As mentioned in the previous section, I never thought one of my employers would change their remote employee rules and allow me to work from home when I relocated to another state, but after demonstrating that I was a top performer, they decided to make an exception and allowed me to stay on with them as a remote employee.

So if a company indicates that the position will end unless you relocate, then I recommend that you prepare to look for other positions but still give 110% in the role as your efforts might pay off in a permanent remote position (or, at the very least, a great recommendation or reference from that employer).

Now, onto the cons of how Covid-19 has affected the remote employment field. First, since many people were laid off completely from their positions, there are more applicants vying for the same roles. However, if you're a great fit for a position, and you demonstrate that in your resume, cover letter, and then in your interview, then you'll most likely move forward in their hiring process.

The issue that's a bit more of a problem is there are so many positions currently being listed as remote, that it actually makes it more difficult to find roles that are *permanently* remote. Basically, this means you'll have to wade through more positions that will populate in your remote job search because a lot more roles mention remote or work from home in their position descriptions. You'll need to make sure you take the time to read each job description to ensure that the jobs you apply for are going to be permanently remote. You'll also need to scan the job descriptions to assess whether you need to live in a specific state or near a specific city in order to qualify for the job.

This definitely adds a little more time to the job search portion of landing a remote position, but if you're willing to take the extra time and carefully read through each job description, you'll be less likely to waste time applying for positions that aren't a good fit in the long run.

Alright, now that we've addressed some of what you might run into in your remote job search during 2021 and onward, let's dig into how to tell a scam from a real remote position, how to most efficiently review a job description, and lastly, where to actually search for legitimate work from home positions.

Scam or Real Job Opportunity?

This is probably my biggest pet peeve when it comes to looking for remote employment opportunities. There are many so-called "positions" out there that are either a waste of your time, have sketchy payment requirements, or are outright scams to steal your information.

Let's start with those pay-to-play jobs. There are legitimate positions with real companies that require a payment to run a background check when you apply for a role with them. I'm not a huge fan of this, but it doesn't mean they're a scam.

However, there are other companies out there that actually try to get you to pay just for the chance to apply. Even if it isn't a scam, this is not worth your money or time. There are plenty of other legitimate, remote opportunities that you can apply for without dropping a dime. Apply for those first and after that, if you really want to apply for a position that requires payment for a background check, circle back to it after you've applied for the roles that don't have a fee.

Personally, I never apply for any job that requires some kind of payment. Jobs are supposed to pay *you*, not the other way around. It's best just to avoid anything that requires some kind of monetary exchange up front.

I also recommend that you not apply for roles that ask for your social security number or date of birth up front. They do not need that information until after you've interviewed and been offered the position. The only caveat to that is if you are applying for a federal position. In that case, you'll apply through the USA Jobs portal (https://www. usajobs.gov) which safeguards that information for you.

Another red flag indicating that a job is a scam is if they ask for your banking information. When you're in the process of applying for a job, they do not need this information. Only after you have been offered and accepted a position should they ask for your direct deposit information in order to pay you.

Lastly, I am always cautious when I receive a "cold" email or message about a job availability. If you've never connected with that person before and suddenly you receive a message about a position that sounds like an amazing job opportunity with pay that's a little too good to be true, then it's probably a scam. Sure, you might get recruiters emailing you with legitimate jobs if you post your resume on job search websites, but if it's a real position, then they'll usually direct you to the company website to apply. Always be cautious when you receive these kinds of messages about jobs that sound amazing. After all, if the position is so amazing, why aren't they posting it where anyone can apply?

We'll dig into this a little more in the next section where we'll focus on how to effectively read through a job description.

What to Look for in Job Descriptions

When looking for remote opportunities, whether you're using one of the general job search sites or a remote-specific job search site, you should always read through the job description. This is not only important to make sure you're a good fit for the position but will also help you weed out any roles that don't fit all of your remote needs.

For example, one thing to carefully look for in a job description is whether or not the role is 100% remote. There are some positions which allow you to work partially from home but require one or more days within an in-person office setting as well. Another detail to look for in the job description is the mention of site-specific training. While some positions might be 100% remote, I see a lot of positions which require you to attend in-person training at their headquarters before the job switches to fully remote. Make sure to look for this kind of thing within job descriptions. Doing so will keep you from applying for positions which you interview for and get offered only to have to turn it down when you're unable to comply with their training or location requirements.

Pay special attention to any technical or environmental requirements, too. While some remote-work employers provide laptops, phones, video cameras, or other necessary equipment, others may specify in the job description that you are required to use your own office equipment and supplies. Some positions might require a certain internet speed or a landline, and other roles might specify that you must be able to work in a quiet space in your home that is dedicated only to your remote position.

When I shifted from a traditional, in-office position to working from home with the same employer, I had to sign an agreement that I would always have the appropriate internet speed required to perform the duties of the position. It's definitely something to be aware of!

Lastly, another important reason to read through job descriptions is that they can tell you a lot about a position either directly or by reading between the lines. Be wary of job descriptions which feel like they are "selling" the job to you. If you find that most of a job description is filled with reasons why that company and/or job is such an amazing place to work, or they harp on all the benefits of the job but don't get into what the position actually entails, then it might not be a great place to work.

I'm also hesitant to apply for a position that hypes up how much money you'll make in the role. You'll typically see this with more sales type positions or for roles that people don't actually want to do. It doesn't mean they're a scam, just that it might be a company with a revolving door of employees because the organization is not great or the job itself is not enjoyable.

After scanning the job description to rule out if it's a scam and ensure that it fits your needs for remote work, the next thing you want to do is review the qualifications. Some employers even break down the position description between required qualifications and desired qualifications so that you'll know if it's worth your time to apply or not.

If you don't have a majority of the required qualifications listed, then that position is unlikely to be worth your time to apply for as you'll likely be up against other applicants who meet *all* of the requirements. However, if you meet almost all the requirements and you also meet many of the desired qualifications, then it might be worth it to take the time and apply.

A good rule of thumb I like to use is to print out the job description (or drop it into a Word document) and then go through it with a highlighter (or the highlight tool in your Word document) and highlight everything listed in the job description that matches your experience, skills, or education. Once you've done this, take a look at the job description as a whole. Were you able to highlight 75% or more of the job description? Great! It's likely worth it to take the time to tailor your resume and apply for the role.

However, if you find that you're only able to highlight 50% or less of the job description, then it's unlikely to be worth your time. Unless it's a dream position and you just want to throw your hat in the ring, then I recommend moving on and spending your time more wisely on positions for which you're more likely to get an interview.

Searching for Remote Work

This can be one of the most difficult aspects of connecting with a great remote position. While searching for work from home positions has gotten much easier now that there are a lot more websites specifically geared toward finding remote positions, there are still a few things you'll want to keep in mind.

. . .

i. Keyword management

Regardless of what job search websites you decide to use, I highly recommend that you get into the habit of maintaining a list of the keywords from your job search. You'll want to track what words work well and give you great results in your job search, as well as the keywords that don't work for you.

A great method is to keep a simple notepad next to the computer as you job search and write down each keyword that you try. If the keyword results in jobs that seem like a good fit, you can use it again on another job search site. However, if you use a keyword that produces zero results or the jobs it pulls up aren't a good fit, then still write down that keyword, but cross it out so you know that you've already tried it and that it wasn't a useful keyword for your search. By maintaining a simple list of keywords that do and don't work, you'll avoid wasting time by continually using keywords that aren't effective.

While searching, also pay attention to job titles for positions for which you're a good match. These job titles can be used as the keyword in your next job search! This will help you come up with new keywords to use in your search and will keep you from spinning your wheels and getting the same jobs over and over in your search results.

Another quick note on job titles: Don't be put off by job titles that don't seem like the right job. Always read the job description before you decide the job isn't for you. Some companies use what might be considered very odd or misleading job titles. Try not to assume anything when reading through job titles because you might skip over a job that would be perfect for you if you'd only scanned through the job description!

. . .

2. General job search websites

Keeping the information from the previous section in mind about scammers and jobs that are too good to be true, you can find some really great job opportunities just by digging through general job search websites like Indeed.com, Ziprecruiter.com, or Careerbuilder.com.

The trick here is that each of these websites has a slightly different method to search for remote positions. For Indeed, you can run a specific job search by typing the job title into the "What" box (the keywords box) and then insert any of the following words individually into the "Where" box:

- Remote
- Virtual
- Work from Home
- Home Based
- Telecommute

If you don't care what kind of work it is and are just looking for a remote job, then try typing each one of those words from the previous list into the "What" box and leaving the "Where" box blank.

With ZipRecruiter, the search for a remote position requires you to type one of the words from the above list into the keywords box. If you try inputting those same words into the location box, you won't get any results.

For the CareerBuilder website, it appears the best method to find remote positions is to input a keyword and the word "remote" (or one of the other words from the list above) into the job title box.

There are plenty of other general job search websites out there, but these are typically my top choices. However, if you prefer a different job search site, you may have to experiment to see what the best method is for finding work from home positions.

3. Remote-specific job search websites

If you prefer to save time by not having to determine if a position is remote or not, you could always try one of the many remote-specific job search websites. The only downside to some remote job search sites is that they either cost money, or you have to wade through a ton of ads to use the free sites. However, it can be worth it as the jobs you find may make up for the time you'd otherwise spend trying to find remote positions on a regular job search site and trying to determine if the position is only temporarily remote during Covid-19 or if the role is permanently remote.

My top website recommendation to use in searching for remote employment has to be Remote.co. This site appears to have been created specifically for the remote work job seeker as it's streamlined to search for virtual positions according to specific industries or using a keyword search. I found it very user-friendly and was easily able to find several positions after one search. I honestly couldn't find anything negative about the site. In fact, this site also has a blog specifically about remote work as well as links for free courses to make you a better candidate for certain positions. So if you're looking for a one-stop shop, I'd start with Remote.co first and branch out from there.

Similar to Remote.co, though not quite as sleekly designed, is JustRemote.co. It allows you to search using keywords or by industry and also has resources for finding remote work and making yourself a better candidate for work from home positions.

Another site you might find useful to search for work from home positions is We Work Remotely. However, it's mainly for programmers, copywriters, developers, and product designers, though they do list roles in customer service and finance.

The next job search site, Pangian, offers very similar roles as We Work Remotely. Though I do like that Pangian lists a salary range for some positions, I don't love that you must create an account and log in to view the full job descriptions.

Next is Virtual Vocations which is a job board that makes it easy to narrow down your search to positions which are a good fit. The only con to this site is that, similar to Pangian, in order to see the position description for roles you're interested in, the site requires you to register and log in.

Another free website for finding remote work is Rat Race Rebellion. This website posts new positions daily and has a list of opportunities (called "The Big List of Jobs and Gigs") which you can search through and apply filters to in order to narrow down the results to specific industries.

However, there are a few cons to this website. The first is that it has a lot of ads you'll have to wade through that are cleverly made to look like part of the website content. The second drawback to this site is that the positions listed aren't just remote jobs but are also gigs and surveys. While there's nothing wrong with picking up gig work or taking surveys in exchange for money or a gift card, be aware that they are not methods of guaranteed, steady income.

Another website that I tend to gravitate toward is Flex-Jobs. While this is a paid job search site, it can be well worth it as FlexJobs vets the positions, allows you to search using keywords or specific industries, and will tell you up front if a position is fully remote or only partially remote. If you decide to try out FlexJobs, you can do a free trial for one week to see if it's helpful to your job search. They have tiered pricing system based off of how long you want to use the service and currently offer one month, three months, or one year plans.

Personally, I think it's unlikely that you'll need their services for a year since it typically takes between three to four months to land a position from the time you start applying. I think the sweet spot for a subscription to Flex-Jobs is the three-month plan since it will give you plenty of time to search and apply for lots of roles.

Note: Regardless of what site you use to job search, I highly recommend that once you find a position you wish to apply for, search for that company's website and apply through their career page (rather than directly though the job search website). This will ensure that your application is received by the company which posted the position, and you won't have to wonder if your application ever made it to the correct inbox.

3

APPLYING FOR REMOTE WORK

You've slogged through the job search process and have found one or more positions that are a great fit—fantastic! Now it's time to shift your mindset into application mode.

In this section, I'll prepare you for some of the surprises you might encounter when applying for remote positions. I'll also explain how to convey information in your resume so employers will be able to see your ability to work independently without close supervision and how you would thrive in a remote environment. Last but not least, we'll go over how to create a compelling cover letter specifically tailored toward remote employment.

Let's start with the fun surprises, shall we?

Surprises in the Application Process

While most remote positions have the exact same job application process as in-office positions, there are some employers who do something entirely different in their application process for their remote positions. To better prepare you, here is a list of a few things you might run across when applying for remote roles.

1. Video applications

You've just hit the apply button for an awesome position at what sounds like a fun company. You upload your tailored resume, and then—Surprise!—the next step asks you to complete a video application.

I don't know about you but having to create a video of myself during the application portion of the process feels a bit jarring. The good news is that, currently, this requirement at the application stage is *very* few and far between. But let's get you prepared just in case.

My recommendation is to treat the video application like an interview. By that, I mean dress up like you would for an interview. Before you hit record, review any information they ask about, then make some notes or fully write out what you plan to say. Personally, I like to make a script and memorize it. Then I create an outline of the script which I post behind the camera where I can see it but the camera can't. This ensures that I'm not just reading from the script (which sounds wooden) but still allows me to stay on track with my mostly memorized script.

Make sure to smile in the video. I know. It's a frustrating recommendation, but smiling makes you more personable, and a hiring manager will be more likely to like you and continue watching your video if you smile and seem likable.

Many application videos allow you to record whenever you want and upload later. The great thing about this is that it means you can edit the video or redo it as many times as necessary.

Something to avoid when creating a video application is just reading from your resume. While it's okay to talk about the experience that's listed in your resume, you don't want to just read down through it, line by line. They'll already have your resume from the rest of the application process. They don't need you to read it to them. Instead, they're looking to get a peek at your personality from the video portion of the application process. Try and focus on answering whatever questions are asked for the video to ensure that you're including in your answers what makes you such a great fit for the position and/or why you love the company. But above all else, follow the directions and ensure that you're answering any questions or prompts provided.

2. Testing and assessments in the application

Though this is not exclusive to work from home positions, you may be required to complete tests during the application, such as typing tests or personality assessments, to make sure you're a good fit for the role. The most common test you'll encounter for work from home positions is a typing test. You'll usually see this kind of thing for roles that require fast typing responses in areas like customer service.

The great news is that you can prepare for this type of test for free! There are a ton of typing test tools where you can see how fast you type. If you'd like to improve your typing speed and accuracy, there are also lots of free typing games which can help you improve your typing skills and are actually fun!

Check out the following free sites to test and/or improve your typing skills:

Speed and Accuracy Typing Tests:

- www.TypingTest.com
- https://www.livechat.com/typing-speed-test/#/
- https://www.keyhero.com/free-typing-test/

Typing Games for Improvement:

- https://www.typinggames.zone/
- https://www.typing.com/student/games

If you need to start at the beginning with typing basics, there are plenty of sites for that as well. Here's one you can check out at:

https://www.typingclub.com/sportal/program-3.game

Another "test" you may encounter while applying for remote employment is less about skill and more about what kind of technical equipment and internet you have. These tests will usually test the speed of your internet as well as the processing speed of your computer.

Don't be put off from applying for other remote positions if you fail one of these tests. Not all employers require high speed internet and many employers will provide you with the required equipment like a laptop. So if you fail one of these tests, just roll on to the next job application.

Resume Tips

When it comes to applying for any job, it's always important to tailor your resume toward the position. This means looking at the job description to determine what the employer is looking for, then ensuring that your resume touches on all the experience, education, and skills that are listed in the job description. Even if you've never held a remote position before, it's likely you've gained some transferable skills at your previous positions which are applicable to working from home.

If you don't yet have a resume, feel free to slide over to my website and download a free resume template: https://www.evergrowthcoach.com/resources.

Also, if you struggle to write a tailored resume and aren't sure you're doing a good job of working in the keywords from the job description, a great tool to use is Jobscan. I love the tools and services on this website, but the thing I use the most on Jobscan is that of pasting a resume and job description into their system and then hitting the scan button to see how well the resume matches the job description.

The results will tell you exactly what hard and soft skills you've left out and will give you a rating of how well you've done in matching the job description. You have to register to use their tools, but once you do, you'll get up to five free scans. I highly recommend using them to make sure you're doing a good job of tailoring your resume toward the job description before you apply.

That said, when applying for remote positions, I also recommend incorporating the following skills and experiences into your resume.

1. An ability to work independently

Working from home is all about working by yourself and staying on task. If you've had some experience working independently before, make sure to include that experience in your resume! This doesn't mean that you just write "able to work independently" and stick it somewhere in your resume. That's telling, not showing, and it won't get you very far with the hiring manager. Anyone can drop, "able to work independently" in a resume, but it doesn't do you much good if you don't back it up with some actual examples.

Show the hiring manager or recruiter what you did by detailing in your resume what task you performed that was independent. If you regularly completed projects or tasks on your own, you might include the following bullet point in your resume:

Regularly completed logistics projects independently with little to no supervision within assigned deadlines with 100% accuracy .

Okay, that was a very generic line. Here's a more specific example. If you completed a specific project, you might say:

Independently spearheaded the customer service department's transition from hardcopy documents to digital documentation and received accolades from management.

Notice how that sentence provides a lot more information to the hiring manager about your ability to work independently. It shows what you did rather than just telling the hiring manager that you're "able to work independently."

2. Able to work without direct supervision

Similar to working independently, it's important to mention any experience you've had which required you to work with little or no supervision. In a remote position, the only supervision you'll encounter is when your supervisor calls or video chats with you to check in. So make sure to include a bullet in your resume about any experience you might have had in which the supervisor wasn't present.

Again, show, don't tell. Instead of "able to work without direct supervision," you might say:

> *Provided janitorial services to three buildings each day and ensured all tasks were completed effectively and efficiently with zero direct supervision.*

Or maybe:

> *Selected from peers to provide onboarding training to new employees and conducted trainings with little to no supervision.*

3. Note when your previous positions were remote

If you've previously worked in a remote or virtual position, make sure that you indicate that on your resume. When employers see that you've had a remote position before, it tells them that you'll be more likely to be successful in the role than other applicants who haven't had a remote position.

To show that a position was remote, you can include the words "remote" or "virtual" in parentheses after the job title. So it might look something like this:

Customer Service Representative (Remote)

This will allow the hiring manager to see right away that you're no stranger to working from home and can handle the unique challenges that a remote employee might encounter. Don't make the hiring manager read your experience bullets to find out that you have remote experience! Always keep in mind that the easier you make it for hiring managers to find the information that makes you a good fit for the job, the more likely it is you'll be brought in for an interview.

Cover Letter Tips

When it comes to applying for a work from home position, including a cover letter can make a huge difference. Not just because it shows what a true professional you are, but also because it allows you to mention any previous remote experience you've had and also whether you have the necessary technical requirements that an employer has listed in the job description.

Because I feel that a cover letter is so important when applying for a remote position, we're going to walk through the process of creating and tailoring a professional cover letter. To get started more easily, feel free to visit my website to download a free cover letter template here: https://www.evergrowthcoach.com/resources.

Let's get started with walking through each section of a cover letter.

1. Add a salutation

If you know the name of the hiring manager or human resources professional that is managing the applications for a position, make sure to address the cover letter to them. This makes the letter more personal, and they are more likely to read it. Sometimes it can be worth doing a little research online to find out who the hiring manager is for a role. One positive aspect of job searching on LinkedIn is that the job description will often state who posted the job description from that company, making it easier to know who to address the cover letter to.

However, if you can't find the person in charge of reviewing the applications for a job, don't stress! It's okay to default to: To Whom It May Concern.

2. Paragraph I

This is where a cover letter for a remote job and a traditional, in-office job will differ. In your cover letter for a remote position, you're going to use the first paragraph to inform the hiring manager what position you're applying for, then you're going to close that first paragraph by letting them know you have the required technical specifications, equipment, and/or quiet workspace.

Remember, the employer has told you in the job description exactly what they are looking for in a candidate. If it mentions needing a certain internet speed and you have that, this is where you'll bring that up. Ditto with having certain equipment or a quiet space conducive to working from home. This is the place to mention those things in the cover letter.

Your opening paragraph might sound something like this:

I was very excited to learn about the remote Data Analyst position with XYZ Inc. and am very interested in applying as I have high speed internet and the experience listed in the job description.

Or

I was intrigued to hear about the virtual Customer Service Representative role at XYZ Inc. as I have previously excelled in remote customer service roles and possess a quiet home office space in which to provide professional customer service to clients.

Notice the main point here is to let the employer know what position you're applying for, then inform them that you have the appropriate technology or experience that the position is asking for. Also, though I refer to this section as a paragraph, it's usually more like one, sometimes two sentences.

Note: This is also a great place to name drop if you were referred to the job by someone who currently works for that company! You could open with something like:

I was excited to hear about the Customer Service Representative position from John Smith, a manager in XYZ Inc's marketing department, and am writing to express my intentions to apply for the role.

3. Paragraph II

The second paragraph will be no different than you would use in a cover letter for an in-person position. This is where you'll mention your strongest reason for being a great fit for the position. It might be because of specific experience from a role you've held or because of your education. Remember: the employer has told you in the job description what they're looking for in a great candidate. Use that to determine what your strongest argument is for being a great fit for the position.

Here is an example:

I feel that I'm a great fit for this position as, during my five years as the only Customer Service Representative at the Button Factory, I regularly worked independently with little to no supervision and was able to improve customer satisfaction year over year using high-touch, personable interactions with customers.

4. Paragraph III

This section is where you'll list your next greatest reason for being a great fit for the job. Again, remember that the employer has told you in the job description exactly what they're looking for in a great candidate. Whatever you mention in the cover letter should directly reflect some piece of information within that job description.

Continuing the Customer Service Representative theme, here is an example of paragraph three:

Another reason that I feel I'm a great candidate for this position is that I am able to develop professional relationships with vendors and business clients. As a Business Client Services Specialist at Zip It Up Manufacturers, I regularly liaised with new vendors while pricing materials and created long-lasting business relationships with third-party sellers.

5. Paragraph IV

In the last paragraph you'll provide the reason that you

want the job. It could be because you want to work for that company, or because you've heard great things about the department, or because in this role you'll get to pursue your passion. This is usually something that you can't really put in a resume because it's a more subjective thing.

I also highly recommend that this be a real reason that you want the job since recruiters and hiring managers are usually pretty good at spotting a lie. Also, it's likely that whatever reason you mention in your cover letter for wanting the job will come up again during the interview. So make sure it's something that makes you truly want the job.

You'll start the fourth paragraph with why you want the job, then you'll close out the letter by quickly summarizing the rest of your reasons for being a great candidate. It might look something like this:

Lastly, I truly believe in creating long-lasting business relationships with clients which aligns with XYZ Inc's mission of creating life-long customers through transparent services and high-touch assistance. This, paired with my experience in business relationship development and improving customer satisfaction while working independently, would allow me to excel in the remote Customer Service Representative role with XYZ Inc.

6. Closing

The last line will be a stand-alone sentence or two before you close the cover letter. Make it something simple like:

I look forward to hearing from you. Thank you for your time and consideration.

Then a few spaces under that, write, "Sincerely" and your name, number, and email address.

7. Review

I highly recommend having someone review your cover letter before you send it. If you don't have someone who can look it over for you, let it sit overnight before re-reading it out loud to yourself. Reading out loud helps me catch any missing words, grammatical errors, or oddly worded phrases.

And always, always, always spell check!

4

INTERVIEWING FOR REMOTE WORK

This is definitely one of the more dreaded portions of the job application process, but interviewing doesn't have to be so bad! The more preparation you can put into interviewing, the more likely you are to move forward in the hiring process.

In this section, we'll cover tips specific to acing virtual interviews as well as recommendations for how to go about answering some of the general interview questions you might encounter.

Tips for Virtual Interviews

Interviewing for remote positions typically requires a virtual or video interview. While this interview, for the most part, will be similar to interviewing for an in-office position, there are a few subtle differences. With that in mind, here are some suggestions on how to prepare for a remote position interview.

. . .

1. Dress up

First and foremost, you need to wear appropriate interview attire for a video interview just like you would if you were interviewing in person for a traditional in-office role. The fact that this will be a remote position actually increases the importance of dressing up for the interview. After all, if you can't be bothered to dress up for the interview, then an employer might feel that you're not approaching the interview professionally and may decide that you aren't a good fit for the role.

And, just to be abundantly clear, please wear pants, a skirt, or something on your bottom half. Just because an interviewer can't see below your waist is no reason not to get fully dressed. Trust me when I say that not getting fully dressed for an interview is just a plea to the universe for something catastrophic to occur during your interview which requires you stand up in front of the camera.

I once had the fire alarm in my home begin randomly blaring its alarm for no reason during an interview. I had to leap onto a nearby desk in order to reach it and remove its battery—all while in direct view of the camera and the interviewer. If I'd worn jeans or something else not interview appropriate, the interviewers would definitely have noticed and it's unlikely I would have gotten an offer that day.

I also once had a client who decided to forgo wearing pants during a video interview. Of course, he forgot this during the interview and stood up to get something at one point, giving the interviewers a clear view of his boxers.

Just... wear some pants, please.

2. Find a quiet, secluded spot

Remember, a virtual interview for a remote job isn't just to decide if you're a good fit for the role and the company, but also to ensure that your home is conducive to getting work done. If you do a video interview where you are constantly interrupted by your pets, children, or other people in your household, an interviewer will most likely assume that you would struggle to focus in a remote position with such a disruptive environment.

To avoid this, let the members of your household know that you're going to be on a video call and ensure that you'll have a quiet, uninterrupted interview.

If getting complete quiet for the interview is an issue, consider purchasing software that dampens or removes background noise from audio and/or video calls. Something like Krisp can be a great tool for creating the illusion of a quiet background on your end of the call. And if you think you'll end up with the same noise issue when you start a remote job, you might consider continuing to use the software for work (if your company allows it).

3. Keep it simple

The space where you'll be interviewing does not have to be complicated. Pick a spot like a desk or a table where you can set down your computer, tablet, or phone (depending on what device you're using to interview). If possible, try to give yourself a little extra room at the table for a pen and paper in case you need to take notes.

Make sure that the interviewer will be able to see you at least from the chest or shoulders up. Look around behind you to ensure that everything is neat and organized if possible. Also, ensure there's nothing controversial or inappropriate in the background.

The simpler the space is, the easier it will be for the interviewer to focus on you and your answers.

4. Ensure tech readiness

Though virtual interviews have much better technology to rely on these days, it's still good to be prepared for some kind of technical issue. Well before the interview (as in days, not minutes), make sure that you don't need to download any kind of software to access the interview platform. If the software the company is using for the interview is free, test it out with a friend or family member the day beforehand to make sure you understand how to use it.

Make sure that you have your phone charged and ready (but on silent) and get a set of headphones ready in case something goes wrong with the virtual interview platform. You never know when you might have sound issues and have to call into the virtual interview rather than use your computer's audio.

5. Lighting and sound

Well before the interview, test the lighting in the space you plan to use. If your face is shaded, grab a desk lamp or a bedside lamp and put it behind (but slightly to the side of) the computer or device you plan to use for the interview. This will give your face better lighting without washing out the picture with too much light.

6. Be ready for glitches

Virtual interviews sometimes experience technical issues or glitches in the software. Don't panic if this happens. The interviewer should be able to give you directions on how to handle issues like a failure of the video platform or audio issues. Whatever you do, don't get upset if technical issues occur. Always assume that the interviewer can hear you or see you, so act accordingly and keep calm during any issues.

Remember, if you're going to be a remote employee, you're likely to deal with technical issues at some point in a work from home position. The best thing you can do if something goes wrong during an interview is to stay calm, take your direction from the interviewer, and follow their instructions. By showing them your ability to roll with the punches and still deliver a great interview, you're demonstrating your ability to be a great remote employee.

7. Keep notes handy

The great thing about a virtual interview is that the interviewer will only see what you show them on camera. This means that you can have a sort of cheat sheet as long as they can't see it. Personally, I like to keep a cheat sheet taped or pinned to the wall directly behind the camera above my computer. That way, if I need to look at it, the interviewer is unlikely to notice since it will appear that I'm just looking at the camera.

And, while I called it a "cheat sheet," you can't really cheat in an interview. The information I usually put in my cheat sheets are things like my top three reasons for being a good fit for the position or why I want to work for the company. I also write down the questions I intend to ask the interviewer, that way I don't forget and I'm not scrambling to try and word them a specific way.

. . .

8. Buy time (if necessary)

One good thing about doing a virtual interview is that if you need to buy time to think of an answer to a difficult or tricky question, you can ask the interviewer to repeat the question because the sound dropped out. This will only buy you a couple of seconds to think of an answer, but sometimes that's all you need. However, I do caution on using this too much as the interviewer is likely to catch on or get annoyed at having to repeat themselves.

Another way to buy time is to say something like, "That's a good question," or repeat the question back to yourself out loud. Again, this will only give you a few extra seconds, but sometimes that's all it takes for you to formulate a good answer.

Tips to Nail Interview Questions

Regardless of whether you're interviewing in person or remotely, it's likely that you'll get asked at least one of the questions below. You don't need to memorize potential answers, but it's at least good to have an idea of how you would answer. Below are some suggestions on what questions to prepare for, but if you'd like more detailed guidance on how to create engaging and realistic answers that will reflect what a great employee you'd be, check out my other book, *Cut the Bullsh*t, Land the Job: A Guide to Resume Writing, Interviewing, Networking, LinkedIn, Salary Negotiation, and More!*

Okay, let's get to the questions you might encounter in an interview.

1. Tell me about yourself

If you do nothing else to prepare for the interview, at least determine how you would answer this question. Time and time again, I've watched applicants trip, stumble, and flail through the "tell me about yourself" question. Almost every interviewer asks some version of this question at the very outset of the interview, so just assume that you're going to be asked to tell the interviewer about yourself.

To prepare for this question, I recommend that at least one day before the interview, write down your answer. This will be 2-5 minutes long and should eventually relate to the position for which you're interviewing. Follow this breakdown to help create your answer:

- 1st Sentence: Basic information about yourself including things like where you're from and education you have that's relevant to the job)
- 2nd/3rd Sentence: Information about the last position you held that's relevant to the position you're interviewing for
- 3rd/4th Sentence: Why you're applying for this position

That it's.

They don't need to know your entire life story. They don't need to know your hobbies, or how many kids you have, or your political or religious affiliations. Just keep it simple and finish with why you want the job.

Here is an example of a good answer to the tell me about yourself question:

After graduating with a Bachelor's degree in Business Administration, I pursued a career in administration and had the opportunity to work in several industries across the federal *and civilian sectors. I found that I was particularly good at organizing and coordinating events which is how I found myself at my last position as an Events Coordinator with the XYZ Events Company. Over the course of my five years there, I was gradually given more responsibility and was granted the ability to work *remotely before being promoted to the Events Team Leader position. I really love working for the organization, but unfortunately there's no room for further growth there, which is why I was so excited to apply for the Events Manager position here at Big Time Events. I really feel that in this position, I'll be able to continue organizing flawless events and create a long-term career here.*

*Notice how this person included up-front that they have remote work experience.

2. Strengths & weaknesses questions

Many employers have stopped asking these questions, but for every one that stopped, there are still a handful who are, not only continuing to ask, but have doubled down and are now asking for two or three of each along with personal examples.

My recommendation is to know at least two strengths and two weaknesses that you actually have. And please, PLEASE don't tell the interviewer that your biggest weakness is that you work too hard. You are not the first person to think of this. Please...just don't do it.

Instead, choose a real weakness you have that won't hurt your chances of getting the job. Then, most importantly, tell the interviewer how you are working on overcoming that weakness. The thing is, if you're a professional and you know that you have a weakness, then you should be doing something to address it. That's the piece that interviewers actually care about.

Here's an example of answering these questions:

Strength:

I feel that one of my greatest strengths is my ability to adapt to ever-changing situations without panicking. For example, at my last position when one of my coworkers was sick, my supervisor selected me to lead a presentation for over two hundred high-level clients and informed me I'd be the presenter only five minutes before the presentation was scheduled to start. I managed to present materials I'd never seen before and even received a few accolades from some of the clients.

Weakness:

I've found that one of my weaknesses is that I sometimes get so excited about the big picture that I miss the finer details. One way that I've been working on this is, whenever I'm assigned a new project, I outline my plan of action and break down my goals into smaller, realistic milestones. Recently, I used this strategy for a new, first of its kind project for updating the organization's entire client database. By working backwards from the organization's overall goal and breaking down the project into smaller, bite-size pieces, I was able to identify and avoid several potential issues before even beginning the project and ended up completing the assignment before the deadline.

Again, keep in mind that your answer to the weaknesses question should always include what your weakness is and what you're doing to overcome it or combat it.

. . .

3. Situational questions

If you've ever interviewed before, chances are you've had to answer a situational question. They usually involve asking you to give an example of when you've experienced a specific type of situation. While I can't tell you exactly what type of situational questions you might encounter in an interview, here are a few that employers tend to like and some that might come up during interviews for a remote position.

- Tell me about a time you got in an argument with a supervisor.
- What would you do if you were working from home and suddenly lost power or your internet connection?
- Tell me about a time you had to deal with a difficult client.
- What would you do if you noticed a co-worker shirking their work duties?
- Tell me about a time you had multiple deadlines and how you handled that.
- Tell me about the project that you're the proudest of having completed.
- Tell me about a time you failed.
- What would you do if you knew that you weren't going to meet an upcoming deadline for work?
- Tell me about a time that you had to make a difficult decision at work.

For each one of these questions, I recommend that you think back to previous positions and try to come up with an answer. If you're given a question for a situation you've never experienced, try to come up with something that's at least close to that situation.

For example, for that first question about getting into an argument with a supervisor, maybe you've never argued with any supervisors, but you might have once disagreed with one. You can say that instead and use that situation as an example.

5

YOU GOT THE JOB! NOW WHAT?

I must say, while I loved switching over to working from home, it was a totally new experience to go from the daily commute and working in an office environment every day to just walking upstairs to my home office. It was liberating...but also a little overwhelming at first when I was suddenly all on my own. After a few weeks, I definitely found myself getting a little lonely without office mates popping by to chat.

I wish I had had some guidance or suggestions to stay focused and keep from feeling lonely when I first started working from home, so here are a few tips to help you get into the swing of things when you first start a remote position.

1. Stay connected to co-workers

Working from home doesn't have to be lonely. If you previously worked in an office where you routinely made a quick round of chatting with your co-workers, you might want to consider connecting with a few of your new remote co-workers. If your company has an orientation of some type (even if it's an online, remote orientation) see if you gel with any of the other employees during that orientation.

When you first start, note the co-workers who have been there a little longer than you and get into the habit of asking them job-related questions. Just like in an office environment, this is a good way to find some personal connections with your co-workers.

Eventually, the goal is to build at least one or two solid connections with your co-workers. Then, just like in a traditional office setting, when you get overwhelmed by a project or just need to rest your brain for a moment, you can reach out to those core co-workers to chat. Of course, just like an in-office job, you're still at work, so keep the chat short.

2. Get into a routine

Whether or not your remote job has set hours, I highly recommend that you adopt a daily routine just like you would for a traditional, in-office position. This might involve getting up at the same time during your workweek, working out, taking a shower, having breakfast, and then starting your work at the same time each day. Doing so will help you be more productive and will keep your body and mind in a steady routine so that it knows when it's time to work.

3. Maintain a separate space for work

As mentioned in the myths and pitfalls in Section One of this book, it can be really helpful to maintain a separate room or area for remote work. If you have a spare bedroom you can convert into a simple office, it can make a world of difference for keeping your work life separate from your personal life. If you don't have the space for a separate room, even just having an area that you designate just for work, like part of the dining room table or a specific chair in the living room, will help you maintain some semblance of mental separation between work and your home life. If you have no space to designate specifically just for working purposes, then get into the habit of packing your work items away at the end of every day. Out of sight, out of mind. Or at least, mostly out of mind.

4. Research tax benefits

Depending on what country you live in, there are some tax benefits to working from your home. I highly recommend that you speak with a tax expert the first year after you start working from home, that way they can ensure that you're taking full advantage of any writes-offs you can take for being a remote employee. You might even speak to a tax expert well before tax season to make sure you're doing everything correctly for tax purposes when it comes to working out of your home.

5. Keep complimentary emails

It's always a smart idea to save any emails that praise your work. These could be from a supervisor, co-workers, or even customers or clients. Create a file where you save these kinds of communications and then you can refer back to these compliments when you are up for performance evaluations.

This could be applied to an in-office position as well, but it's especially important for a remote role since you're unlikely to meet in-person with a supervisor or co-workers which means it can be a little more difficult to make a lasting impression.

6

CLOSING

Taking a work from home or remote position can be a truly liberating experience. Sure, you still may have to work a regular shift, but cutting out that terrible commute and not having to deal with someone else's smelly lunch or annoying habits in the office is pretty wonderful!

But don't take it from me—follow the suggestions in this book and land a remote job to see for yourself!

7

RESOURCES

To make things a little easier, I've rounded up all the useful resources that have clickable links so you have them in one location.

General Job Search Websites

- https://www.Indeed.com
- https://www.Ziprecruiter.com
- https://www.Careerbuilder.com
- https://www.Monster.com

Remote Job Search Websites

- https://www.Remote.co
- https://www.JustRemote.co
- https://www.WeWorkRemotely.com
- https://www.Pangian.com
- https://www.Rat Race Rebellion.com
- https://www.FlexJobs.com

Speed and Accuracy Typing Tests:

- www.TypingTest.com
- https://www.livechat.com/typing-speed-test/#/
- https://www.keyhero.com/free-typing-test/

Typing Games for Improvement:

- https://www.typinggames.zone/
- https://www.typing.com/student/games

Useful Tools

- Jobscan – Allows you to compare your resume to job descriptions. Sign up for five free scans to make sure your resume has all the keywords from the job description. https://www.jobscan.co
- Krisp.ai – Need a quieter background for interviewing or for a remote customer service job? Krisp can mute background noise in many communication apps, that way your interviewer or customers don't know there's a barking dog or screaming baby in the background! https://krisp.ai/

Resume & Cover Letter Help

If you need a little more in-depth guidance on creating a cover letter and/or resume, you can download free templates under the Resources tab on my website: https://www.evergrowthcoach.com. You'll also find my guide there,

Cut the Bullsh*t, Land the Job, which takes a much deeper, step-by-step approach to creating a tailored resume and includes 25 resume examples and five cover letter examples.

I also offer resume writing services at three payment levels so you can choose the service that best suits your needs. And soon I'll offer low-cost courses for those who prefer a more visual step-by-step approach to finding, applying, or interviewing for positions as well as how to be a great employee who receives promotions.

If you'd like to stay informed about what resources I have available and hear about upcoming books or free promos, join my newsletter here: https://www.evergrowthcoach.com/subscribe-landing.

ABOUT THE AUTHOR

Jennifer has been helping job seekers discover how to get more out of their job search process for over seven years and has assisted clients from a variety of industries at all leadership levels. Her Master's in Community Counseling was the perfect base upon which to build a career in employment coaching as it honed her ability to listen attentively and pinpoint her clients' job search struggles before identifying actionable solutions that landed them the job.

You can learn more about Jennifer's career services and access free career tools and resources by visiting: https://www.evergrowthcoach.com/

ALSO BY JENNIFER JELLIFF-RUSSELL

Cut the Bullsh*t, Land the Job is an all-inclusive guide to identify why you're not getting your dream job and will walk you through the process of fixing the problem. With simple, step-by-step instructions, this book will cut the bullshit from the job search process and show you how to:

• Job search effectively and find the roles you want

• Create a killer resume and tailored cover letter that lead to job interviews

• Build a professional network and get job referrals

• Develop an eye-catching LinkedIn profile that captures recruiters' attention

• Nail interviews with impressive, high-impact answers

• Negotiate the salary you deserve

...and more!

AUG 1 2 2023

9 781734 284669